Reflec

RAINBOW
PUNCH

Edited by Lauren A. Hayhurst

Reflections on Lockdown

RAINBOW PUNCH

Edited by Lauren A. Hayhurst

palavro
PUBLISHING

Rainbow Punch

By Lauren A. Hayhurst

© Lauren A. Hayhurst

ISBN: 978-1-912092-43-7

First published in 2024

Published by Palavro, an imprint of
the Arkbound Foundation (Publishers)

Arkbound is a social enterprise that aims to promote social inclusion, community development and artistic talent. It sponsors publications by disadvantaged authors and covers issues that engage wider social concerns. Arkbound fully embraces sustainability and environmental protection. It endeavours to use material that is renewable, recyclable or sourced from sustainable forest.

Arkbound
Rogart Street Campus
4 Rogart Street
Glasgow, G40 2AA

www.arkbound.com

For Alicia and Arlo

**For all
lockdown babies
and those who helped them thrive**

~

Thank you for purchasing *Rainbow Punch*. All the royalties from this sale go to Rainbow Trust Children's Charity, a charity which supports seriously ill children and their families. Lauren, editor of *Rainbow Punch*, has two babies, Alicia and Arlo, who both needed to spend time in the neonatal unit when they were born. For this reason, Lauren wanted to give something back by helping others survive the hardest of times.

In aid of

RAINBOW TRUST

SUPPORTING FAMILIES
WITH A SERIOUSLY ILL CHILD

INTRODUCTION

'What's lockdown mean?' my three-year-old asks, whilst trying to do a headstand on the sofa. Her baby brother has just nodded off in the swing - a fancy moving cradle, complete with six speeds, white noise or music, and even a vibrating seat. I'm attempting to sneak a few minutes writing. It's slow progress.

'Well, lockdown happened when you were born and... everyone had to stay at home.'
'Why?'
'Because there was a bug outside making lots of people poorly.'
'A spider?'
'No, a teeny tiny bug called a virus, so small you can't even see it.'

I tell her how we weren't allowed outside except for a short walk each day, and everything was closed so we couldn't get cake at the café or go to the library or soft play.

'Do you want to see a picture of you?'

I show her the website I created in May 2020, when she was just six weeks old - lockdownbabybabble.com - and she's entranced by the artwork and the words and the photo of her looking out of the window, and that lasts all of five minutes before she tries to muscle-in on the keyboard to play 'work.'

RAINBOW PUNCH

*

I've thought about these conversations a lot since she was born, how I might explain lockdown, how to communicate the surreality of the situation. Now, in 2023, I'm not sure that's even possible, but it feels so important to try and this anthology is the result of my efforts.

Whenever lockdown gets mentioned now - for me it's usually at mum and toddler groups snatching adult conversation in between 'Are you sure you don't need a wee' and 'Yes there are more snacks' - most people struggle for the right words, me included. We might share a baffled laugh or glaze over, lost in memories that might as well be from another dimension.

Casting your mind back to this time is likely to stir up difficult feelings. Whatever stage of life we were at, whatever our lockdown living situation, whatever the specifics, we all experienced drastic and rapid change, which is a struggle for most people. Despite this, when the subject comes up, there's always a spark of connection, maybe because existing through that time gave us all something in common; we survived something significant, even if we don't know how to talk about it.

I hope this anthology helps in this regard. Because along with the shared struggle, we had rainbows. As symbols and images go, the rainbow is a popular one, inviting a multitude of interpretations thanks to their rarity, vibrancy, and variety, punctuating a period of volatility with a sense of calm. The

LGBTQI+ flag might come to mind, representing hope and inclusion within a community. In Greek mythology, Iris is a goddess of the rainbow, connecting humanity to the gods. In the Bible, a rainbow appears to Noah indicating safety and renewal after the great flood. Rainbow babies are those born after a loss, bringing life, love and healing to their loved ones. Then there's the rainbow bridge where beloved pets are said to wait for their owners, whilst Dorothy in *The Wizard of Oz* finds her dreams 'somewhere over the rainbow.'

The adoption of the rainbow during lockdown was not dissimilar to these examples of hope, community, connection, renewal, and healing. The trend of placing rainbows in windows started in Italy but ricocheted across the world; a silent squeeze of solidarity sent across empty streets, windswept parks and their creaking swings, captured in the glances of those timed walks, and carried back to lonely homes, perhaps inspired to invest in their own creations and amplify the good feeling.

As we entered the second UK lockdown in November 2020, it was comforting to have the same rainbows accompany our walk, beaming out from the privacy of unknown living rooms, a visual hug from strangers saying to an anxious, new mother, 'hey, you got this, keep going,' and I could relax my grip on the buggy and breathe. As we entered the third lockdown in January 2021, those same rainbows, now faded and forlorn, still managed to punch through any fretful reverie. In daydreams, I knocked on front doors and complimented the artwork and showed off my baby and smiled at the kids

indoors and made new friends and got invited in for tea...
In reality, I simply smiled and continued walking, but I had
these daydreams, I had hope.

*

I manage to wrestle the keyboard off her.

'Can I read you something, poppet,' I say, recapturing her
attention. 'Can I read you something mama wrote when you
were a baby?'
'When we lived with Granny and Grampy. When I was a tiny
baby, like baby brother.'

How does she remember this stuff? I must have only
mentioned it once before. 'That's right, you clever thing. You
ready, you comfy?'

I read her my poem 'Beyond the Horizon', which prompted the
lockdownbabybabble website and subsequently this anthology:

> One day, my darling love, I'll take you
> beyond the horizon.
>
> We'll dance with the sunshine wherever it leads.
> You'll see tree families walking tall together,
> clouds of leaves whispering in the breeze.
>
> You'll see where land's edge has spilled the sky
> and water gushes forever.

You'll feel the ground give way beneath your toes
in playful sandy softness. You'll breathe
in the salty sea freshness and feel
its rough residue on your skin hours later.

You'll be in my arms, windswept but warm,
a bundle of snuffles and sleep that I'll keep
cosy and close for as long as I'm needed.

One day, my darling love, I'll take you
beyond the horizon.

But for now we'll stay safe inside.

She loses interest by 'tree families' and escapes my embrace in favour of her toy house. I ahem away clichéd tears and finish reading with my eyes fixed on baby brother, asleep and still swinging.

*

We got the swing during the first lockdown, when my daughter was a few weeks old. It was the height of excitement as far as her limited new experiences went.

In contrast, the first four weeks of baby brother's life were filled with beach visits, sand between his toes, waves lapping at his skin. He blinked at baboons and yawned at rhinos at the zoo, lay on the grass at the park and enjoyed cuddles from countless people.

RAINBOW PUNCH

There's something in this poem, in the snapshots captured - the longing, the uncertainty, the hope - that seems to clarify how precious these achievements are. That we might never see the beach or the park or kiss and hug friends ever again, felt like a totally tangible possibility and regardless of how ridiculous that seems in retrospect, I can still feel this fear tightening my skin, halting my breath. And yet, experiencing my second motherhood in freedom brings an unexpected perspective.

Other mums talk about actually enjoying lockdown with a baby, wasn't it nice, they say, not to have to go out. I could not fathom this at all, I was desperate to be out in the world as a new mum, going to baby clubs, sharing lack-of-sleep stories, meeting for coffee in the park. Because of this, I was determined to make the most of my maternity leave the second time round, so in the first few weeks we barely had a day at home. Then, I suddenly get it, that gratefulness for being forced indoors.

All the early experiences I had with my son, whilst exhilarating and uplifting and fulfilling, have also made the time pass much more quickly, which is no good thing if you're trying to savour every second of a rapidly changing baby. This realisation brings a new appreciation for lockdown with my daughter. Being forced to a physical standstill seemed to slow down time, so from this perspective, lockdown amplified focus on the smaller details and elongated memories of that precious period. Having come to this realisation, slowing down and focusing in is something that I now consciously incorporate with my son. Of course, recalling difficult aspects of lockdown may provoke a fear response, but it is possible to also look to it for transformation.

Every piece selected for *Rainbow Punch* encourages reflection in this way, taking a difficult aspect of lockdown and inviting contemplation through a transformative rainbow prism. Every piece is illustrated by one of six artists, each bringing their unique style and insightful interpretations to enhance the writing, inviting deeper and more nuanced contemplations with every read.

Many writers explore community and connection, such as in Canwell's piece where story rainbows are draped around the streets, manifesting the brotherhood featured in Davidson's haiku. For Dheda, a connection is made only during the pandemic, even after aeons of searching, and it is due to the pandemic that Arana's experiences such deep connection with an online friend. Sanders conveys the rainbow's ancient power for connection and suggests how remembering less favourable times can amplify the good. Pattnaik also embraces this act of remembrance by recalling those lost to the pandemic, as does Borgersen, whose protagonist pays tribute to her late friend by embracing the colours that she loved so much.

Renewal features through the healing qualities of a downpour, as Kenny and Nedhal explore, and just as the Earth is cleansed, so is the soul, in Jasat and M. Pearson's contemplations of new motherhood. Such hope is echoed by Clayton, Hawke and Kendall, as they share the intimacy of pregnancy and newborn days, whilst maternal courage arguably reaches its climax in Pearson's story, where the protagonist escapes an abusive partner to secure her young daughter's future.

Just as rainbows signify a move outwards towards safety, so too does Lee recognise the need for freedom to nurture development. This emphasises the importance of comfort and encouragement when freedom is limited, which are portrayed as essential survival tools by Meyer-Currey and Barnes. With these tools, we may recover from the suffering, but, as Duffy demonstrates, a part of us will remain forever changed by this time.

*

It's another day and we're at Daddy's house. We've just finished tea - veggie sausages and mash, yogurts for pudding, one apricot and one raspberry - and now we're in the front room. There's not a lot of space, one sofa for sitting, the other covered with toys - cuddly friends, puzzles, play-food, magnet maze - and the floor is covered in Duplo, wild animals, books.

Baby brother gurgles in the bouncy chair, sneezes. Alicia stops loading up her trolley.

'Mama... What's lockdown mean?'
'Well,' I take a sip of tea, 'we talked about that the other day, didn't we, can you remember what we said?'
'No, I not 'member.' She abandons the trolley and comes to squeeze between me and Daddy.
'Okay, well it happened when you were born...'

'When I was a tiny baby, like baby brother.'

'That's right, and everybody had to stay...'

'Home.'

'Because there was a...'

'Coz there was a bug outside, but, but, it wasn't a spider.'

'Can you remember what it was?'

'I not 'member.'

'Well, it was a virus that made a lot of people poorly.'

'That's why we had to stay home.'

I nod and she thinks for a second, then she goes over to her nest of wooden Night Garden blocks and tips them upside-down. They clatter abrasively and I cringe, but let it go, conscious of allowing her train-of-thought to continue uninterrupted.

She brings the blocks to the sofa two at a time and we shift up to make room, watching as she lies them sideways. They're hollow, the blocks, so like this they make good cubby-holes or caves. Then she fetches the animals, choosing carefully. The shiny sand-filled creatures, lobster, squid, snake; plastic elephant and tiger, giraffe; two tiny ornaments from the mantlepiece, a turtle and a lion, wooden with nodding heads.

'Here you go,' she says. Daddy gets the lobster, me the elephant. She starts to place them inside, one animal per block. 'See? We playing lockdown.'

My surprise quickly melts; of course she would turn this into a game. Toddlers thrive on mimicry and my daughter loves to re-enact whatever she sees me doing. It never would have occurred to me back then, that the isolation, the longing and uncertainty, could become distilled into something so innocent as a child's game.

For those who don't remember or weren't there, this book can provide a glimpse at what lockdown was like. For those who did live through it, I hope this book will encourage new ways of looking at otherwise difficult experiences. Just as my daughter's game of 'lockdown' simplified the issues through playfulness, I hope this book can also generate some unexpected positive gains. For everyone willing to remember, I hope this book helps you heal and grow.

Lauren A. Hayhurst
August 2023

REMNANTS OF NIGHT'S TEARS

SHANNON KENNY

Round midnight the sky drew a veil of cloud across the moon and stars, blocking all light from our distant suns.

And the sky mourned like only it could.

In an instant, a flash of lightning scarred the heavens, and a crash of thunder echoed the cry of a billion bereft hearts.

Near and far, in homes and offices, hospitals and refugee camps, villages and cities around the world, hearts were waiting and bending and breaking.

By morning the sodden earth could not contain all that the sky had poured out, and the remnant of the night's tears covered the ground in little pools reflecting clear blue and birds on the wing in silhouette.

On the horizon, a few clouds clung to the sky while an ocean breeze wafted over our city.

Wishful thinking - or hopeful wonder - lifted our eyes and spirits as the sky-prism drew its colour-arch and reminded us of a time before we were locked down and locked in; before we had to assure a loved one that the bee-keeper zombie at their bedside was one of the good guys in the story; before we were afraid of what we could not see; before the eyes became our only window to another's soul - that hearts bend and break and mend.

'Remnants of Night's Tears'
Illustration by Shireki

SCATTERED LIGHT

JODIE DUFFY

A stop sign. The climbing curve on the graph. A line on the ground, not to cross. Danger. Caution.

The orange paint on her palm and the prints on the paper. Brightness slapped on the page. Optimism. Get ready.

Sunflowers stooping in pots on the patio. Dandelions in the cracks in the pavement. A stay-at-home summer.

Grass under our bare feet. Our garden, our oasis from boredom. Hedge boundaries. Hope. Life: organic, instinctive and imperfect.

The blue NHS logo on the news, on posters coloured with crayons. Discarded disposable facemasks. Motorway signs. Distance.

Ink. Plans crossed out. Rearranged, crossed out again. My name, written on a vaccination card.

Fallen petals. The lingering bruise of lost time. Like a rainbow, it too will fade into the horizon, but flare in our memories.

'Scattered Light'
Illustration by Terri Bate

RAINBOW'S END

KATE MEYER-CURREY

All through lockdown I saw it:
a rainbow sign, thanking us
healthcare workers. It caught
my eye, on the last turnoff
before the hospital. Like us,
it was there every day, rain
or shine. No choice
but to tough it out through ward
lockdowns, short staffing
or the brief respite
of our vaccination appointments.
As time wore on, its bold
PPE colours faded,
its edges curled,
ready for the clinical
waste bin, bone-tired
after another sweaty shift.
It kept up its lonely vigil
for us
all winter, standing
on its roundabout doorstep,
a solitary hand-clap
lost in the wind. Like us,

its bright optimism
dimmed to a shadow
of its former self, dulled
by the year's restrictions. Its hope
so much fool's gold:
empty rhetoric spouted
by government officials
about what great work
we were doing. Spring
came but the sign
had gone. So I thought,
until I drove home, one day
in March, dodging showers
and glancing sun. Then
I saw another rainbow
had taken its place, cheering us
on; banishing monochrome clouds
into quarantine with renewed
prismatic assurance.

RAINBOW PUNCH

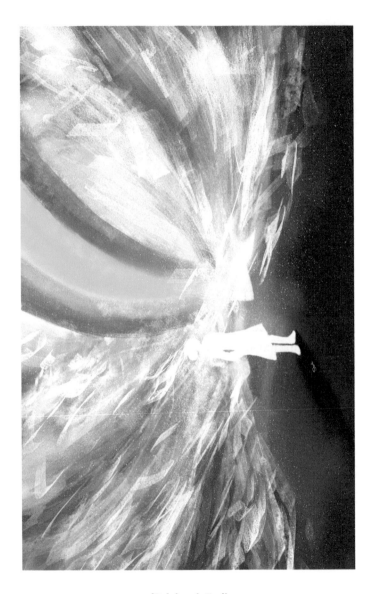

'Rainbow's End'

Illustration by Shireki

THE COLOUR OF COURAGE

LAURA M PEARSON

The first rainbows appeared a week or so after the first lockdown started. Slowly at first, until within a month, every other house featured a colourful arch: hand and fingerprints, painted brush strokes, collages, cut outs, chalk murals, knits. Beautiful, imperfect, unique.

In our street, the first rainbow was in my next-door neighbour's window - a large arch with a small red handprint beside it. I smiled and messaged to say we loved her picture. That is what these rainbows were about - bringing a wee bit of happiness and making a connection, communicating with all these strangers living beside us, going nowhere. Talking through pictures. *Have hope* we said, *stay strong. We will get through this together. We are following the rules. We want to be safe together, here.*

I arched a red line and my two-year old's shaky hand copied underneath. I bit my lip. I wanted to tell him there's no black in a rainbow, encourage him to make his shapes rounder and taller, make his rainbow perfect. Instead, I watched his face - concentrating so hard on those wobbly lines, loving his authority in selecting the next colour, joy at sticking his artwork up in our window then rushing outside to see how it looked. I promised silently that I would get him through this.

RAINBOW PUNCH

We walked our dog every day and as we daundered round the streets we looked for new rainbows in windows. I remember being out one sunny morning and coming across a sign that brought my stomach to my throat: 'we're isolating'. The curtains had been drawn. My eyes burned with tears, and I tried to hold them back. My brain conjured up visions of what might be on the other side. Zombies. Thank goodness this virus did not cause the mutations of horror films. My instinct was to post a note and offer help, but ashamedly I was too scared. No-one we knew had yet been confirmed with Covid and we fluctuated between stockpiling paracetamol and Calpol, and disbelief.

Around me, people were clearing out garages and renovating gardens, but I could only focus on getting through each day. I was so grateful to have my son. I had started a long career break a year earlier, so I didn't have to juggle working-from-home and childcare. I could give him all my attention, and, despite the unfamiliarity of lockdown and isolation, I enjoyed that time together.

So many mum-friends were having tough times. Working-from-home while looking after toddlers and pre-schoolers; a whole new level of mum-guilt. We were all buckled on to this Covid rollercoaster, but we braved additional rides of personal circumstance: bereavement, anxiety over vulnerable relatives, kids with allergies, distance from family, work pressures, relationship problems.

I boarded my own rollercoaster five weeks before lockdown started, when I woke one morning after a vivid dream of being pregnant. The sensation was so strong, feet pushing my stomach from the inside, it stayed with me long after waking. As a believer of signs and coincidences, I let this dream take over my thoughts and dared to imagine the possibility of a baby. While my son and husband went swimming that afternoon, I went out and bought a bottle of wine and a pregnancy test. The wine remained in my fridge.

When I saw those double lines, I whooped in joy and disbelief to an empty house. I was desperate for my husband to get home. As I waited, my rollercoaster started clack-clacking up the steep slope - fear kicked in - would this baby make it? This little bundle of cells was our rainbow baby. We had lost his big brother the year before, at our 20-week scan, and our hearts had been shattered. This little baby was a symbol of hope. As I waited for my family to return, I used my sternest voice to tell this baby he was to hold on tight and that we already loved him immensely and wanted to meet him properly.

I could never have expected that only five and a half weeks later I would be googling 'impact of Covid-19 on unborn baby.' We found little in the early days. A study from China said five pregnant women with Covid gave birth to healthy babies; a new-born baby in London who tested positive for Covid but seemed to be doing okay. My husband took emergency annual leave from his keyworker, public-facing job, which gave us a week to consider our options. We poured over medical websites. I could isolate at home, but we were terrified of my husband bringing Covid back and infecting me and the baby.

RAINBOW PUNCH

With this, and all the general Covid uncertainty, my anxiety continued to rise. The NHS guidelines meant I had to attend all antenatal appointments and scans alone. I was under the care of the local foetal medicine team and the two midwives became like friends during my pregnancy. They passed me tissues as I sobbed under my facemask. They were, and are, my heroes. They let me cry, pour out my experiences of losing my son the year before, and nodded when I voiced fears for the baby I was carrying. Then they gave me the strength to make it to my next appointment. They sealed the sex of my baby in an envelope for me to take home to open with my husband and son. They managed appointments so that my wait time in public areas was minimal, but they never rushed me out of the consulting room. They were my lifeline and, other than my husband and son, the only people I saw during the first lockdown.

On so many days I felt sure my baby was gone, that his stillness meant I had lost him. When I next went to hospital, I prepared for the worst. But at every check, his heart pounded out like a runaway train and flooded my body with relief. The little fella enjoyed partying hard for three days, then resting for three. I recognised his pattern and relaxed. It helped to have a toddler keeping me busy, and as my tummy grew, he seemed more interested in the baby brother he would soon meet. We had been honest with him about the death of his brother the year before, and many times he would ask 'is this baby going to stay and live with us?' Tears pricking my eyes and throat tight, I responded with the only honest answer, 'I hope so, darling.' We would tell the baby how much we loved him and how much we wanted him to come and live with us instead of going to heaven like their brother had. And we would hope.

Though the anxiety of losing our baby was unwavering, and at times intense, in many ways lockdown made the pregnancy easier. I didn't have to tell people as soon as I started to show. I was glad to avoid strangers asking about my bump. I didn't want to answer good-natured and happy questions. I didn't want to tell people his due date, show his scan pictures, or talk about his birth. I didn't want people to say this baby would help me 'get over' the loss of his brother. It wouldn't. I didn't want people to know how hard it was to imagine him as a baby and not see the face of the baby we lost, still and silent.

I don't think I properly relaxed until he was safe in my arms, and I kissed his beautiful face and fingers over and over, thanking the stars for the breath in his lungs and his beating heart. I had to spend three nights away from my toddler as he wasn't allowed to visit us in hospital. The happiest moment of my life was walking out with my beautiful baby and seeing his big brother and dad waiting for us outside, waving and grinning in the cool October twilight. I have never felt more blessed and more complete. I sat in the back seat, a son on either side of me, fingers entwined with each and cried tears of joy the whole way home, my husband watching me in the mirror. We did it.

Now my rainbow baby is nine months old. My older son has learnt to ride his bike. Unfortunately, my beloved dog passed away. We have not lost anyone to Covid. We like to go for cycles and when we do, we still see some rainbows up in windows. Curled at the edges, paper yellowed, colours faded by the sun. Some renewed with fresh, vibrant hues, or even replaced with more permanent versions, fabric or glass. And as I see them, I wonder if these symbols depict what it means to be human, to travel as both individuals and a collective, a unique mix of souls all joined by this common rollercoaster of life. The downs may cause our hope and positivity to crinkle over time, but the ups enable us to renew the bright hope we carry inside. And whilst we never know what ups or downs wait around the next corner, we still ride on with courage.

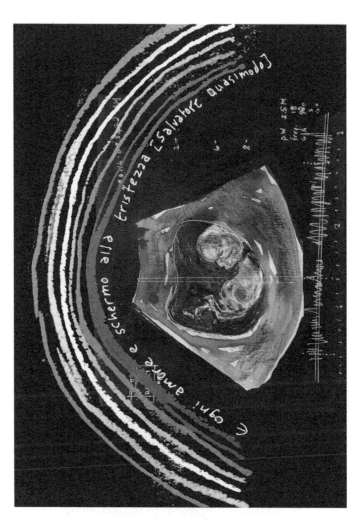

'The Colour of Courage'

Illustration by Silvi Judd

A HAIKU IN LOCKDOWN

TRACY DAVIDSON

rainbows appearing
in neighbourly brotherhood...
ornate windowpanes

'A Haiku in Lockdown'
Illustration by Anne Pass

COLOURING BY WORDS

RACHEL CANWELL

At the beginning, her neighbours hoard toilet rolls, stash pasta and paracetamol galore. The panic of plenty is everywhere and no one knows the meaning of enough.

But her mind is far away, beyond these things. Her eyes are falling only on the words. Every day she lifts them, wrapping each one with skill and care. Collects and polishes, buffs them to a gentle shine.

And one by one she holds them up to the unexpected, endless sun. Turns them through the light as each word reveals its own unique hue. From scarlet to violet, turquoise to teal, the words slowly leech their colour, seeping and spilling across her desk.

Wonder and admiration make her strong. As the world recedes, she pulls the words in closer, her only constant company.

Amid the silent fear that grows denser every day, she begins to weave, seeking harmony and hope. She treats each word as a broken gem, and with care and love, slowly, piece by piece, she threads them all together, watching the stories come.
Each one is a tapestry, a whole made up of fractured, disparate

light. Combinations that have come together, colliding, sudden, vibrant, and beguiling, bursting from the page. They wink and call to her from all corners of the room. She writes without stopping until her world is alive with their possibilities, the walls and floors dazzling with constant and refracted colour.

And before long, the tales she's created are too demanding, too beautiful to be contained within this house.

So, she takes to grabbing them, a handful at a time, a thousand different shades spilling through her fingers. She folds each page, stuffs them into pockets and sets out. In her allocated thirty minutes, she moves through silent streets. Leaving her lexicon of rainbows all about the town. Sometimes as she hurries on, she glances back. From over her shoulder or the corner of her eye, she sees someone retrieve her words. And from a distance she will pause, watch them read and see the colours arc. Observe pairs of tired eyes flicker with the spark of shared experience, a face, a life, suddenly and safely seen.

The words she conjures paint the lives of people she has never met. A thread of light and colour that soars in unity across the town.

People whisper that she is a magician.

She simply calls herself a writer.

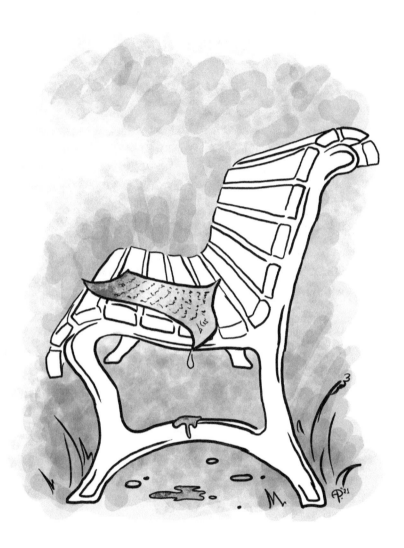

'Colouring by Words'

Illustration by Anne Pass

HOPEFUL HUES

ELLEN CLAYTON

Rainbows adorn windows as we walk
A skittle shot of dopamine
In a terrifying time. Come summer, we must
Navigate an uncertain world of masks and two metre rules
But the rainbows remain, a different hope
Of a life growing in my womb after loss.
Walking through town, I imagine colourful bursts of joy
    willing you into existence

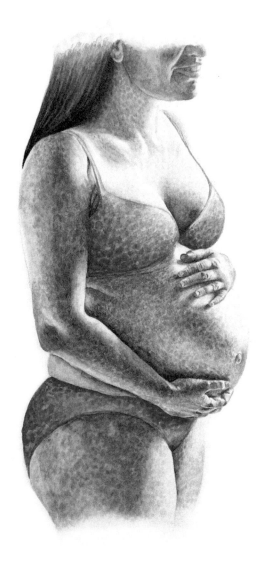

'Hopeful Hues'

Illustration by Amy Briggs

WAITING FOR THE MAGNOLIAS TO BLOOM

SARAH M JASATOOLA

The late dawn has barely taken hold when I open the curtains and peer into the back garden. It is March, and the trees are still bare, the grass patchy and muddy. Last night the Prime Minister was on TV again, talking about his roadmap, his way out, but I was thinking of this garden, the only source of life where most remain dormant: the magnolia tree growing up against the fence. I squint at the tiny buds that have formed in the last week on its branches. Are they a fraction bigger than yesterday? Most are still green, but there are a few on the south side that are beginning to tease white hearts and my gaze lingers, as though by staring I can will them to turn pink, to swell and burst open.

It doesn't work. The buds remain hard nubs of green no matter how long I look. But I remind myself as I turn away from the window, they are there now, were not there a month ago, and a month from now, who can say?

'I can't do this.' It was not so much the words as the wavering hysteria in my voice that made my husband look up from his phone.

'What's wrong? Do you need help?' He joined me at the kitchen counter where I had assembled a group of ingredients for a simple pasta and vegetable sauce. It was a dish I had made many times. I knew how to make it, in theory, but in my mind it suddenly seemed like an uncrackable puzzle. I couldn't fathom the flavours or imagine how it should taste. I wanted to cry.

The sickness arrived at the end of November, before my missed period and the two lines on the pregnancy test. It hung around me like a grey cloud, fogging my mind, sapping my strength and leaching all previous pleasures from my life. It accompanied me through every moment of waking life and sometimes chased me into my sleep.

I sat on the sofa and held my head in my hands, listening to my husband work in the kitchen and trying to beat down the wall of hopelessness that was welling up inside me. I was, even by generous calculations, only a few weeks pregnant. At the least I could expect two more months of this, but it was likely to be much more. I grabbed a pen and on the back of an envelope worked out when I could expect the first trimester to end, my already uneasy stomach twisting tighter as the dates seemed impossibly far away. Twelve weeks seemed optimistic, I thought, so I factored in an extra month and landed on the last week of March.

'That'll be the beginning of Spring. Hopefully lockdown will be easing by then too,' my husband said when I showed him the calculations. His plate was clean. The few forkfuls I managed were threatening to creep back up my throat. 'Something to look forward to.'

The grey cloud is my constant companion. It weighs down each step as I walk to the bus stop, it steals my breath when I stand for meetings, it sends me crawling into bed as soon as I get home and crying while I throw up in the toilet or sink or shower. There are things I used to enjoy, I remember, and I try to remind myself. Reading books. Watching dramas. Going for walks. Riding my bicycle. I worry about the amount of plastic going into landfill, and the lack of pollen for bees. People around me talk about variants and cases, deaths and hospital beds. On rare days I muster enough energy to take a short walk, seeking distraction from my own misery. The shops are all still closed. There's nothing to buy, no-one to talk to. Everyone has a harried, closed-up look to their faces.

I pass a couple walking their dog. 'Feel like I'm at breaking point,' the woman says, and I want to nod, and hug her and scream because I am there too, I can't bear another day of this, another hour or another minute, but I must, I must. We all must.

I was staring out of the window, willing the cloud to break for just a moment and let the sun through. I remember sun. Things were better, when there was sun. I felt better, I remember, but that was so long ago. Through the window, I looked at the bare branches, so cold and skeletal against the sky, and then noticed the magnolia tree. It was bare too, but along its branches, I saw the tiny round buds, proof that time wasn't standing still, that we wouldn't live like this forever, that someday soon there might be colour in the world again.

My phone said magnolias bloomed at the end of March. I dug around in my bedside drawer and found the envelope I had scribbled on all those months ago. I held onto it until it grew dark, and I fell asleep.

I have never watched anything as I watched this magnolia tree. Most years, I noticed them flower, but never as I did this year. First, the buds grew and turned white, then they began to loosen, revealing deep pink, almost shocking amidst the still grey skies. First, one flower, then a handful, and one morning I woke up to find the whole tree covered in pink and white blossoms.

'Spring,' I said to the window, and though the grey cloud was still there, I realised it wasn't as strong as it had been. I realised I had the energy to go downstairs, open the back door and go outside. I stood beneath the tree and let my eyes drink in the colours.

Now it is June, and I sit beneath the magnolia tree, making different calculations and wondering when you will be ready to join me here. The pink and white blossoms have long been shed and in their place the branches are heavy with glossy green leaves. Even so, the garden is a rainbow of colour with pink and yellow roses bobbing along the fence, purple foxgloves popping up in the borders and rhododendrons so full of scarlet flowers that the stems can hardly be seen. I sit and drink it all in beneath a faultless blue sky. Amidst the birdsong and buzz of the bumblebees I hear children laughing and the sounds of my neighbours chatting. Just like the garden, the world has opened up again.

Inside, I feel your movements. Tiny limbs unfurling, growing in strength each day.

I count the months and weeks and imagine sitting here with you in my arms. It may be some time, but I have learned how to wait.

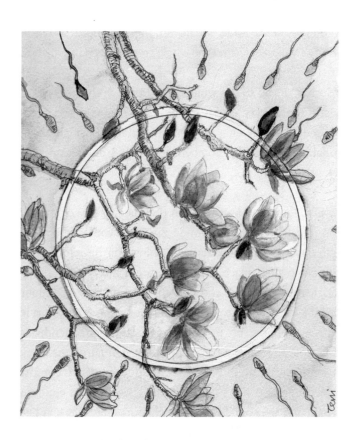

'Waiting for the Magnolias to Bloom'
Illustration by Terri Bate

THEN AND NOW

SEBNEM SANDERS

Restless in lockdown
ailing with disinformation
inside the flat
nothing seems as before.
Bold? I used to be, sometimes,
other times a coward.
Where have the dreams gone?
Remember the good days,
a dip into the sea, when it was allowed,
idyllic picnic on the beach to welcome the full moon.
Nature's gifts to inspire the soul,
beholding the scenes in memory's pixels.
Over the hills, a rainbow is forming,
while spring showers try to wash away the pandemic.
Ready to get the best shot on the mobile,
as the colours become clear under the sunshine,
I click on the camera and forget the worries for a minute.
Nothing is as bad as it seems,
behind the fears, some hope can still be found.
Oleander trees are blossoming again.
With the climate change, summer comes early.
Resting on my chez longue on the balcony,

and mixing memory with the moment,
I savour a cocktail of images.
Noir and blissful,
beloveds, the sweet and the sour.
One and the same,
without one how can the other exist?

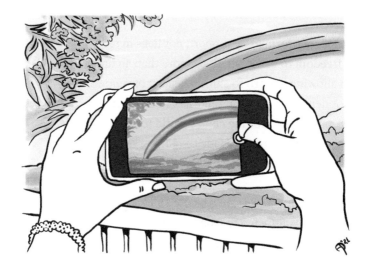

'Then and Now'

Illustration by Anne Pass

DRAWING PARALLELS THROUGH A DOUBLE RAINBOW

EMMA LEE

Resilience formed by support, not flags in red;
a freedom to make her globe more than an orange
in allowing her orb to shine a beacon of yellow
not deny her talents in tendrils of soft green
brought a need for my child's world to be a calm blue,
obstinately refusing to fade to indigo
while my memories are bruised violet.

While my memories are a bruised violet
obstinately refusing to fade to indigo
brought a need for my child's world to be a calm blue,
not deny her talents in tendrils of soft green
in allowing her orb to shine a beacon of yellow
a freedom to make her globe larger than an orange
resilience formed by support, not flags in red.

LAUREN A. HAYURST

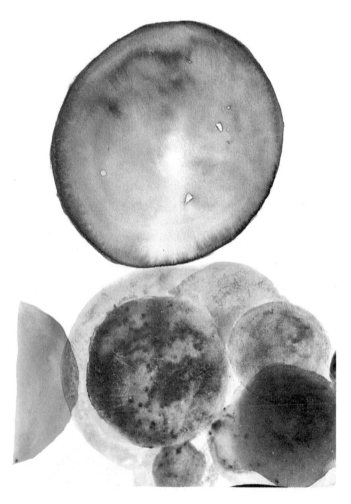

'Drawing Parallels through a Double Rainbow'

Illustration by Silvi Judd

BRIGHT, BEAUTIFUL AND BOLD

SUE BORGERSEN

'Red?' said Amanda, reacting to her friends in a voice that should have been more subdued. 'You know red's not my colour.'

'Amanda. Stop. Listen to yourself. Red is just an idea. This is what she wanted. Right? Bright. Beautiful. Just like she was when she was alive. We all owe this to her. Just colourful then?'

Amanda was a jeans girl, always was and always will be. But for Larissa, her best friend and ally, she would forget the jeans for once and wear a dress. And a colourful one at that. Larrissa had loved her, was always there for her. And Amanda loved Larrissa right back. She still couldn't accept her bff was gone. Taken just like that. Snatched. A victim of the pandemic.

'Nothing for it then,' she said. 'Stores are opening up this week. I'll go shopping. Bright. Beautiful. Will do.'

Amanda bought a dress. She wasn't inspired when she saw it on the rack, 'like curtains', was her first thought. 'But, for you, Larrissa, my love, I'll do it,' was her second.

The dress was bold, as well as bright. She tried it on. Twirled. Watched in the mirror as the yellows, oranges, viridians and purples flashed like psychedelics before her eyes. Amanda swallowed in disbelief at the jungle print's peacock blues and greens of exotic birds. 'You look like a million dollars,' wowed the sales assistant.

Amanda didn't want to look like a million dollars. Didn't want to be giving her bff 'a good send-off'. What she really wanted more than anything in the world, was her bestie back.

That night Amanda slept in the dress. She dreamed that she and Larissa were cruising the Caribbean, trekking through Peruvian jungles, dipping naked into the Aegean, and sipping brandy sours at their favourite bar.

'Bright, Beautiful and Bold'

Illustration by Terri Bate

WHAT LOVE IS

LAURA PEARSON

Rainbows in every window, their colours bright and bleeding. Alice drew one, the tip of her tongue poking out of the side of her mouth in concentration. I searched around for something to stick it up with, settled on tape even though I knew I'd pay for it. Nervously attached it to the window while she looked on, proud. By the time he came home, I'd forgotten all about it. Our tea was ready, and I was standing by the sink, draining the carrots. When he came up behind me, punched the side of my face and left my ear ringing, Alice was standing in the doorway, silent. Always silent.

I thought about all the things she'd seen, over months and years. What she'd remember. How she'd think this is what love is, if I didn't do something.

'What the fuck is this tape doing on my window?'

His window. Mine when it needed cleaning. He was pulling it down, and I saw Alice's lip tremble when the picture tore in two. She wouldn't cry, though. She knew better than that.

'I just thought...'

He was back at my side in an instant, and I stopped talking, shut my eyes against him.

'Fucking rainbows,' he said.

We ate in silence, Alice's head hung low over her pork chop.

It wasn't the first time. Wasn't even the first time that week. A small voice whispered that it could be the last.

Later, when he'd gone out on his bike, I cuddled Alice on the sofa, hoping my love would cancel out his anger.

'We could leave,' I said, testing it out.

Her eyes flicked to meet mine. 'Where would we go?'

'I don't know,' I told her.

I thought about my mum, the house I'd grown up in, the distance between us that couldn't be measured in miles. My dad, just an older version of him. Why hadn't I been able to see it? Would Alice be the same?

I stood, remembering. In the pocket inside my jacket, slipped into the seam so he wouldn't find it when he went rummaging, there was a card. A phone number. An escape. I'd been embarrassed when the receptionist had first handed it to me at the surgery, but her eyes had been kind, and I could tell she'd seen the marks and bruises for what they were.

'Get your things,' I told Alice, trying to keep my voice steady. Gentle. 'Some clothes and Rabbit.'

She slipped past me, determined. I watched her reach for the pieces of the rainbow picture and carefully fold them. Perhaps there was still time, for her. Perhaps she could learn a different way. I thought of how she'd looked up at me in the hospital, when they'd laid her on my chest. How I'd promised to be the best mum I could be. I pressed the numbers with shaking hands. Had to do it twice. But then, a voice. Soft and kind. Asking if she could help. And I was on the floor, the tears I'd held in for all those years suddenly freed, saying yes, saying please, saying help.

'What Love Is'

Illustration by Anne Pass

COLOURS

SHIKSHA DHEDA

I see you drenched in gold -
I feel conscious of my silver being.

I have searched for years
    - even in the darkness –
in the colourless sterility of this
isolated pandemic. Searching.

Always
    - for a colour to revere, worship
and love.

Oh, the electric blue was delightful!
But at times, so very demanding.

The emerald green looked promising,
but turned out to be too stable
for my malleable metallic soul.

Yellow was so close to you,
but its brightness brought
much disturbance to my sombre vision.

Then there was matte black.
Strong, solid and deep. Its darkness
overshadowing; not complementary.

Finally, I have found you.
My incorruptible, sincere, shiny
supportive gold;

so compatible
that I wonder how I've bore
so many aeons without you.

We shall remain together,
   - entangled:

my silver head against your golden shoulder,
your sparkly gold lips atop
my moonlit forehead.

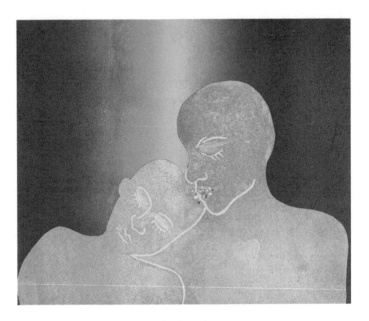

'Colours'

Illustration by Charlotte Hawke

CANDY MOM

AMY BARNES

Reaching upward, we grab spinning rainbow wheels of penny candy from the sky: pink cotton floss, sour lime green, citrus yellow, cinnamon red hots, blue raspberry swirled sticks to lick. Always pressed against iridescent sky glass, not at the counter with glass jars of hard discs and soft taffies and crunchy caramel toffee; we order bulk bags that arrive by mail. Inside the house, I keep boxes of sweet things, treat things, to erase that we are stuck inside -- dogs, children, spouse. Never entering mall candy stores with candy barrels to pick out fancy candy or gum or sticky things to strike fear in the dentist's hearts. Being in a pandemic year is not sweet, but we've made it sweeter.

One child licks the sunset sky. While the other one spins the rainbow illusion with one finger. I pull each pastel and bold bit of rainbow into my pockets and save them for later, when it's raining or normal or Tuesday or March. I'll line up the memories, sweet and sour and sugary and broken and serve them up -- a year's rainbow in a day.

'Candy Mom'

Illustration by Amy Briggs

A SPECTRUM OF COLOURS

SEBNEM SANDERS

When she saw the rainbow in the skies over Gaia,
She didn't know she would soon be going to Leia,
to meet the aliens on the Pink Planet,
and wash away her tears when ample time was granted.

Time like the colours of the rainbow,
starting with red, orange, and yellow,
blending on to green, blue, and indigo,
reflected in the crystal skulls of the Mayan window.

Inca, Aztec, Maya, the indigenous cultures,
worshipped the rainbow before the white vultures
descended on their calendars and ripped off their treasures,
leaving them only with memories of their secret pleasures.

Sunshine through the rain makes a rainbow,
forming ribbons of colours in the skies of sorrow,
inspiring mankind to use this natural wonder of reality,
as a symbol for human expression in solidarity.

Rainbow flags fly in the skies over Gaia,
the colour spectrum same as in the memories of the Maia,
uniting everyone in a natural phenomenon,
oneness inspired in its embrace for all that is human.

RAINBOW PUNCH

Alas, we have now stepped into a new phase,
fighting with a virus and its new vocabulary,
pandemic, social -distancing, vaccines, quarantine,
lockdown, and the extraordinary.
My thoughts are with you through this ordeal,
I can see you on the screen, hear your voice,
and though you are not near
I'll remind you of the rainbows and everything we hold dear.

'A Spectrum of Colours'

Illustration by Charlotte Hawke

PALETTES OF A PANDEMIC

SHALOM ARANAS

In the Bible, the floods came. Ours is of a different nature. The air is flooded with viruses so malevolent, it mutates parallel to vaccines, as though it knows. The children are kept inside, and the photos of them painting rainbows on their glass windowpanes are heart-breaking, so I decide to write.

Red is the colour of love. Such optimism, such hope, so fragile are these rainbows struck by the light of the sun.

Orange is the colour of what the men and women wore while packing vaccines in boxes. I watched YouTube videos of them, packing these vaccines for the first recipients across the world. They clapped and I felt a tumultuous beating in my heart at the hope from these little vials placed carefully in boxes and poured with ice. They were rolled into vans and aeroplanes with much prayer and fervour.

Yellow is the colour of happiness. Four years ago, I met a gay Arab online. We became friends, and when Covid hit, we chatted happily on Facebook. I told him I have a boyfriend, a beautiful Indian, but that he fell obsessively in love with my former nanny. He said, It's okay, it's okay, and I felt as though I had laid my head on his lap, and he was caressing my hair, because life is such as it is. This kind gesture during a pandemic made me feel as though he were a father to my inner child.

Green is the colour of our farm in Tagaytay. I first encountered the idea of an inner child in one of my prayer group's therapeutic retreats. I am a lapsed Catholic, but I eavesdropped on their testimonies, fanning myself on a chair while my sister, mom, and friend Joycelyn participated through Zoom in our farm on Tagaytay. I wondered about my own inner child and how far-gone I am from how I started in life. I am fifty now, with two grown-up kids. I was bullied as a child, and so I loved summer vacations much more than the daily quotidian life as a student. This meant riding ships back to my grandparents' ancestral house. I recall the heavy smell of fuel and oil. We would peep into the waves lapping the bottom of the ship, and I could see the iridescent colours of the rainbow on the oil sap of the ocean.

Blue is the colour of my illness. I have Bipolar Mood Disorder, but the thing is, despite my condition and that my husband left us, I managed to raise my children. I vowed to make their childhood happy. I vowed they would go out. We frequented resorts and fun play-places all over the area of Alabang where we lived. When that phase of my life was like a blue swimming pool, I turned it to a rosy pink and a mild palette of yellow, like the sun after the rains.

Indigo is part of my daughter's palette of colours. Her identity apart from mine. I am no artist, and I do not think in terms of colours. But my daughter is a whole other story. She would join painting contests and win prizes. Her drawings were a crazy pink with indigos and magentas and a myriad of other colours. She drew characters like Leonora Carrington with a cast who were surreally out of this world: pink flowers, roses, blue unicorns, elephants with trumpets as trunks. They were beautiful and astounding like a call to the world to be more imaginative. And yet she was just enjoying herself, happy to be given a generous collection of paints and canvases.

Later, she would design our farmhouse and astound us with her sophisticated choice of colours and materials. The farmhouse was built in haste, and we would go there on weekends. We took off our masks and face shields to relish the fresh air of the mountain. I also happened to transfer residence with my son, and so my daughter and I were designing our new homes at the same time. I wrote voluminously of vampires, angels, and mad caliphates and their poor queens, as well as experimented in alchemy and used a scent called Neroli as a character for my novels. We created where there was emptiness, where we could only see viruses, but also, if we looked hard enough, the kindness of strangers amidst death and the detritus of disease and decay.

Violet is the colour of vaccines. There is an aeroplane being loaded with boxes. Everyone is about, watching with bated breath yet joyful, tearful, clapping. The hind mouth of the aeroplane closes, and it is steered by the pilot across the tarmac. It gathers energy, and slowly it runs, runs faster then finally ascends to the sky. Later it will land, and the vaccines will be distributed. Are we saved? We look to the blue heavens, find our inner parent, and if we're lucky to have survived a bad childhood or to have had a good one, God smiles upon us, and the vaccines will work.

'Palettes of a Pandemic'

Illustration by Anne Pass

NEON LOVE

GEORGINA KENDALL

Rose-gold is the glow of the sunrise,
The very first dawn of your life.
You curl on my chest, in our hospital bed.
Me, dazed, but up on cloud nine.

Aquamarine is my birthstone,
a gift, late last night.
'It's like a blue cloud,' he showed me.
'In there, your thoughts can hide.'

Indigo-blue are your eyes,
when they first peer up at mine.
Light just dim, night beautifully quiet;
they glow deep and vital and wise.

Neon love, I am overwhelmed.
I see you, the mayhem is gone.
We scatter a million light rays,
Creating a radiant bond.

Blush and flush and rush to my cheeks,
I feel angels are near.
Searing heat, their bright wings beat.
In my awe, I draw strength from fear.

RAINBOW PUNCH

Orange burn of the fire,
In the evening by estuary tide.
I pause as I move and gather my strength,
For I know that tonight you'll arrive.

Wild blue yonder,
I'll show you our view of the sea.
We will sail, we will dream, we will wonder,
You, your daddy and me.
We'll light fires that will glow in our hearts,
To the back of beyond.
You were born on the First of September
In the year of the Rainbow, my son.

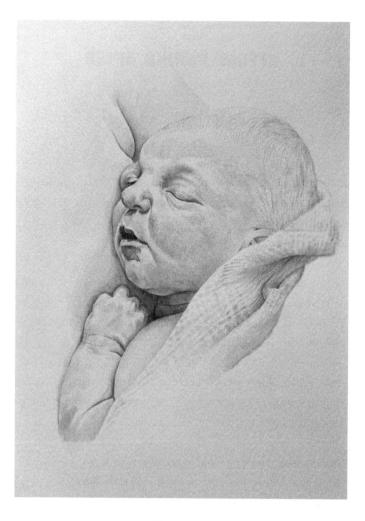

'Neon Love'

illustration by Amy Briggs

BEFORE, DURING, AFTER

CHARLOTTE HAWKE

Red was the line that Basquiat drew; short, sharp, exciting
Red became the wavy line that wound into my arm, new blood
for the half I lost
Red is the strawberry smushed into your podgy face.

Yellow was the glinting patchwork that covered Klimt's
twisted bodies
Yellow became my bag of piss that someone else emptied
Yellow is the rubber duck bobbing in your bath.

Pink were the flowers that O'Keefe painted, so calm and so smooth
Pink became my eyes when lockdown meant they couldn't visit us
Pink is the colour of clothes you receive.

Green was the land of Goldsworthy's organic art
Green was lost in the frost of my hospital window
Green is the grass we sit on studying crispy fallen leaves.

Orange were the life jackets hung by Ai Weiwei
Orange became the colour of all food on my plate
Orange is the bright backbone of my book that fascinates you.

Purple was the skin -tone of Francis Bacon's portrait
Purple became the bruises left by needles in both of us
Purple are the petals you try to eat in the garden.

Blue was the pigment Yves Klein patented
Blue was your tiny, swollen face when you were born
Blue is the fresh, open sky that looks over our lockdown-
free future.

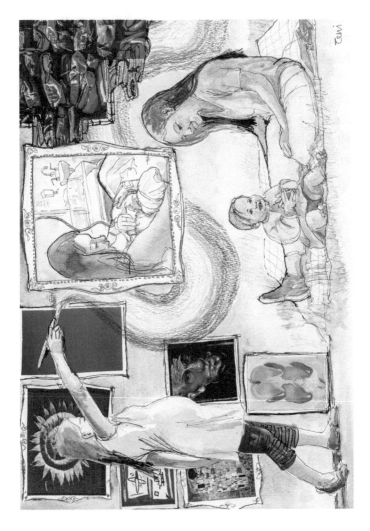

'Before, During, After'

Illustration by Terri Bate

AFTER THE RAIN

CHRISTINE NEDAHL

Running through green fields
After heaven's mead has doused the earth
In diamond sparkles on every frond
Now set free from hidden chains
Blessed with a freedom
Over time denied
Wasted lives never forgotten.

'After the Rain'

Illustration by Silvi Judd

RAINBOW TOMORROW

MANDIRA PATTNAIK

Remembrances of how you shuffled about with a baby at your hips while home-schooling your toddler boy, and how you scoured stoic libraries bereft of readers for books on times like these, and, finding none, sulked for a planet as helpless as yours.

Again, on afternoons like this, recall how you painted rainbows, upturned them like sunshine smiles on your windows, like all the other mothers waiting here, under the billowing banners for the school parade.

In minutes, the crowd of eager parents swells, the babble rises, for here comes the celebration.

No masks, no distances or suspicious glances when you mingle with Brett's mother and Sally's granny, and Tara's mother and sister, shoulders brushing for the first time since the virus was defeated forever.

Before the parade, the anthem plays, a song of the planet, common for your race; trumpets, drums, even a banshee and sitar join in.

RAINBOW PUNCH

Over the hills, the music rolls, no eye is dry, you won, learning you won't ever be left alone. Learning what it is to feel entwined with more of your species.

With the crowd chanting, your boy emerges with his class, all in pretty bowties and smart uniforms, matching steps to cheers under confetti showers, wishing for lasting happiness and peace.

Together, after the ceremonies, you take the public bus; your boy licking a strawberry ice-lolly, you imagining the barbeque waiting to surprise the kid back home.

On the sidewalk, as the bus whizzes past, there are remnants of the times: shutters down and crooked, cloth masks strewn about. It'll take time to get back again, as the news people suggest.

Monday, you'll visit the cemetery where fourteen of yours lie. Some died for want of emergency medicines, some for lack of treatment, some never made it to hospital.

Orange-hued skies welcome you at the bus stop, the neighbourhood park all lush and green, filled with the force of being alive, on the verge of wilderness.

Ronnie would be fifty-six today, a brother you missed, and Laila, your son's teacher, and her daughter Shareen of the NHS, if they saw the restoration of the planet... if they lived to see...

Rusted knob creaks when you open the door. Your boy enters first, smells the heavy-hanging barbeque smoke, 'Ah! Roasted chicken!' he exclaims. 'I'll set the table,' you say, and rush inside.

On the balcony, your boy is already waiting when you present the home-baked dark chocolate cake, a little plate of your favourite fries, cherries and sugar candies, the colours tinging the clouds above, complimenting the flavours of this special day feast.

Whatever happened, all that you endured and won, remaining resilient against the odds, you hold all this dear, and as you watch the boy savour the meal, you finally feel happy within yourself.

RAINBOW PUNCH

'Rainbow Tomorrow'

Illustration by Silvi Judd

BIOGRAPHIES

Amy Barnes lives in Tennessee with her kids and dogs. She has pieces forthcoming at The Citron Review, The Sunlight Press, JMWW Literary, Janus Literary and Cease, Cows. Her full-length collection of short fiction launched in March 2022 from word west press. Find her on Twitter at @amygcb.

Amy Briggs lives and works as a teacher in Fife, Scotland. Becoming a mother transformed her art practice, focusing her work on what it means to be both a mother and a woman. She primarily paints portraits and nudes, drawing inspiration from her own experiences of pregnancy, breastfeeding and beyond.

Charlotte Hawke is a Bristol-based artist and educator who took up writing as a therapeutic tool whilst looking after her daughter during lockdown. She teaches art to young people and to adults facing disabling barriers. Her writing has been published in the Born in Lockdown project, and her artwork can be viewed at www.charlottehawke.co.uk and on Instagram @chawke111

Chris Nedahl, retired from teaching in the Rhondda Valley, South Wales, to live in the Almanzora Valley, Spain, 14 years ago. Writing is her joy - about anything and everything. Flash fiction and poetry are current favourites. She has been published in a number of anthologies and online.
https://christinenedahl.wordpress.com/

Dr Hedge is an alter-ego hedgehog. She was born and raised in Tallinn, Estonia. By day, she teaches game theory at a UK university; by night, she enjoys creating illustrations and crafting superhero costumes for local conventions.
@hedgytimes on Instagram

Ellen Clayton is a poet from Suffolk, England, where she lives with her husband and three young children. Her poems have been published in various print and online publications. Her debut chapbook, *Home Baked*, was published with Bent Key Publishing in April 2022. More of her work can be found on Instagram @ellen_writes_poems.

Emma Lee is from Leicester, UK, and is a writer, editor, and reviewer. When not doing any of those, does embroidery, chiefly blackwork. Her most recent poetry collection is *The Significance of a Dress* (Arachne, 2020), and she blogs at https://emmalee1.wordpress.com

Georgie Kendall lives on the Plymouth estuary, where the River Plym meets the Ocean. Sunken barges, tanker ships and sea birds offer an odd mix of beauty and industry. She's happiest on a bike, in a river or digging up a garden. She also loves to write, capturing emotions and memories.

Jodie Duffy lives in Gloucestershire with her husband and daughter. Much of her poetry is inspired by motherhood and everyday life. Her poems have been published in a number of online and print publications, including Capsule Stories, Free Verse Revolution and Blood Moon Journal. You can find her on Instagram @chrysanthemum_poetry

Kate Meyer-Currey was born in 1969 and moved to Devon in 1973. A varied career in frontline settings has fuelled her interest in gritty urbanism, contrasted with a rural upbringing. Her ADHD also instils a sense of 'other' in her life and writing.

Laura Pearson is an author who lives in Leicestershire with her husband and children. When she isn't writing, she's reading, eating her kids' chocolate and complaining about being tired. Her novels are *Missing Pieces*, *Nobody's Wife*, and *I Wanted You To Know*. You can find her (always) on Twitter at @laurapauthor

Laura M Pearson lives in Fife, Scotland, with her husband and two sons. She absolutely loves being a mum but loves it slightly less at 2 am wake-ups. She has always loved books and dreamt of being a writer when she was wee.
Say hello on Twitter @laurapearson77

Lauren A. Hayhurst is a writer, mother, educator and storyteller. She completed her PhD in 2018 exploring the ethics of representation for fiction writers, and since then has lectured in creative writing and narrative design. She has recently taken a break from academia to conduct fieldwork in baby-rearing and imaginative play, but can be found sea-swimming every chance she gets. A quick Google will reveal published poems or stories, but Rainbow Punch is her first book publication and she's extremely proud, doubly so having achieved this during her matrescence.

Mandira Pattnaik (she/her) is a writer from India. Her work has appeared in over 150 journals/magazines in 15 countries, including Best Small Fictions Anthology 2021, Passages North, Amsterdam Quarterly, DASH Literary, and Lamplight Magazine. She enjoys writing columns for Reckon Review and Trampset. Find her at mandirapattnaik.wordpress.com and on Twitter @MandiraPattnaik

Rachel Canwell is a writer and teacher living in Cumbria. Her flash collection, *Oh I do like to be*, was recently published by Alien Buddha. She is currently working on a novella in flash and her first novel, which was shortlisted for the Retreat West Pitch to Win 2021. Her short fiction has been published in Sledgehammer Lit, Pigeon Review, Reflex Press and The Birdseed, amongst others. Website - https://bookbound.blog/writing/. Twitter - @bookbound2019

Sarah M Jasat writes short fiction exploring the strangeness of family. She lives in Leicester and enjoys riding her bicycle and eating packs of Cadburys fingers in one go, not always at the same time. She dreams about writing a children's novel if only she could get her own children to go to sleep. Sarah tweets @sarahmjasat

Sebnem E. Sanders lives on the Southern Aegean coast of Turkey and writes short and longer works of fiction. Her stories have appeared in various online literary magazines and two anthologies. Her collection of short and flash fiction stories, *Ripples on the Pond*, was published in December 2017. https://sebnemsanders.wordpress.com/

Shalom Galve Aranas is based in Manila, Philippines. She is interested in found objects, second-hand books, movies, music and literature. She has been published in Synaeresis, Minnie's Diary (nominated for the Pushcart Prize), The Blue Nib, Enchanted Conversations, Prachya Review, and elsewhere. She is a loving mother of two.

Shannon Kenny is an actor and writer. She is especially interested in the uncomfortable truths that sneak up to challenge what she thinks she believes. Shannon, an incurable optimist, lives in Durban, South Africa, with her husband and daughter. Featured in the following publications: 100 Words of Solitude; Rejection Letters; Lockdown BabyBabble; Janus Literary; The Manifest-Station. Twitter: @ShannonKenny031

Shiksha Dheda is a South African of Indian descent. She uses writing to express her OCD and depression roller-coaster ventures but mostly to avoid working on her master's degree. Sometimes, she dabbles in photography, painting, and baking lopsided layered cakes. Her writing has been featured (on/ forthcoming) in Wigleaf, Passages North, Brittle Paper, Door is a jar and Epoch Press, amongst others. She is the Pushcart-nominated author of *Washed Away* (Alien Buddha Press, 2021). She rambles annoyingly on Twitter: @ShikshaWrites. You can find (or ignore her) at https://shikshadheda.wixsite.com/writing

Shireki is a student born in Switzerland and raised in three different cultures, German, Chinese and Swiss. Having been in a love-and-hate relationship with art for many years, she has recently found some closure and started to enjoy the process of drawing again. Her medium continues to grow from 2D to 3D. She does commissions and can be contacted on Twitter @Shireki1 and Instagram @shireki.

Silvi Judd is an illustrator, photographer, creative arts counsellor and Adoption Social Worker in private practice. She does art therapy with adopted South Africans whom she assists in tracing their birth family and origins. For more information, go to https://www.adoptionreunion.co.za/. Her art portfolio can be found at https://nightfishing.co.za/

Sue Borgersen lives and writes in Nova Scotia, Canada, where she enjoys beach walks with her dogs and knitting socks. Recent books: *Fishermen's Fingers* (novella), *While the Kettle Boils* (micro-fiction), *Of Daisies and Dead Violins* (poems), and *Eva* (novella). Her publisher is Unsolicited Press. www.sueborgersen.com

Terri Bate was born and still lives in Devon, UK, having lived in Wisconsin, Wales and London in between. For many years she worked as a midwife, retiring nine years ago. When her dog died, she cycled to Australia solo and knit and spun and drew a picture daily for the 17 months she was away. Since the pandemic, Terri continues to knit, spin, draw, and paint from home and is once again owned by a dog.
www.tutleymutleytextiles.com Instagram: @tutleymutley

Tracy Davidson lives in Warwickshire, England, and writes poetry and flash fiction. Her work has appeared in various publications and anthologies, including Mslexia, Writing

Magazine, Modern Haiku, Artificium and In Protest: 150 Poems for Human Rights. Apart from writing, Tracy enjoys reading crime fiction, music, theatre and travel.

ACKNOWLEDGEMENTS

Thank you to the incredible Arkbound publishers, to Riyan, Zoe, to the board of trustees for seeing the beauty of these pieces and for investing in such an unusual artefact. You have been extremely patient whilst I had baby Arlo and settled into my second motherhood. Thank you for understanding how difficult it is to progress art alongside two time-consuming little humans, and for being so flexible with my mental health complexities and requirements.

It was a long journey of learning on my path to finding Arkbound, and I'd like to recognise the kindness of a few people along the way: Maddy from Birch Moon Press, Marcelle from Rare Swan Press, Isabelle from Fly on the Wall Press, Ashini from Dandelion Revolution Press, and Anna from the Cheltenham Literary Festival. You all took the time to respond to my queries and offered sage advice to this publishing novice. Your encouragement helped me continue in my quest to find the right home for this labour of love, and your kind words spurred me on through the long nights of toddler wake-ups and working cross-eyed on my phone.

I owe a massive amount of gratitude to my parents, Jan and Tom, and my partner, Simon, who listened to my woes, made astute suggestions and lived through lockdown without mentioning the ludicrousness of my starting this project. And of course, my two heart-melting babies, Alicia and Arlo, who continue to shape my world and bring meaning to existence. Thank you to all the thoughtful and generous backers to our crowdfunding campaign, without you this book would not have happened, and I hope you all enjoy seeing the finished article.

Finally, thank you to the fantastic Laura Besley and Haley Jenkins for their time and expertise in guest judging and editing the collection. And of course, all the incredible contributors for volunteering their time and talents towards this project. I felt so connected to you across the world, thank you for sharing your slice of life and for your never-ending patience and belief. Thank you for accompanying me on this creative journey throughout life's challenges and celebrations. We got there!